Cherokee Legends and the Trail of Tears

From the Nineteenth Annual Report of the
Bureau Of American Ethnology

Adapted by

THOMAS BRYAN UNDERWOOD

Includes

The John Burnett Version of The Cherokee Removal

Courtesy of
The Museum of the Cherokee Indian

Cover Design and Illustrations
By AMANDA CROWE

Published by
Cherokee Publications
P.O. Box 256, Cherokee, North Carolina

Other Publications:
  The Story of The Cherokee People
  The Cherokees Past and Present
  The Magic Lake
  Cherokee Fun and Learn
  The American Indian Cooking and Herb Lore
  The Arts and Crafts of the The Cherokee
  American Indian Prayers and Poetry
  The American Indian Coloring Book
  Please Don't Step On Me
    (An Indian ecology book for children)
  Indian American
    (A Geography of North American Indians)

(WRITE FOR FREE CATALOG)

1st Printing 1956	10th Printing 1973
2nd Printing 1958	11th Printing 1974
3rd Printing 1960	12th Printing 1976
4th Printing 1961	13th Printing 1977
5th Printing 1963	14th Printing 1979
6th Printing 1965	15th Printing 1982
7th Printing 1967	16th Printing 1984
8th Printing 1969	17th Printing 1986
9th Printing 1971	18th Printing 1989

19th Printing 1991

CONTENTS

How The Earth Was Made

THE INDIANS believe that in the beginning all living things lived and dwelled above in the sky—Galun' lati. Which was above the sky vault. But after awhile the sky vault began to be crowded with all the people and animals. Finally someone asked what was below the ocean that they could see from their home in the sky, and at last Dayuni'si, "Beaver's Grandchild," the little water beetle, offered to go and see if it could learn. When it flew down from the sky vault it darted in every direction over the surface of the water, but could find no firm place to rest. The water beetle dived to the bottom of the ocean and brought up some mud which began to grow and grow. It grew and spread on every side until it became the island which we call the earth. It was afterward fastened to the sky with four giant ropes, but no one remembers who did this. Not even the oldest of the oldest medicine men.

At first the earth was very flat and soft and wet. The animals were very anxious to get down to the earth so no one would be pushed off the sky vault, so they sent out different birds to see if the earth was dry enough to live on. These birds flew around over the earth until they grew very tired but they could find no place where they didn't sink up in the soft mud. All the people and animals were very discouraged, but after a long while they decided that the earth had dried enough so they sent out the great buzzard. Now this buzzard was not an ordinary buzzard. He was the grandfather of all buzzards. He flew all over the earth, low down near the ground, and the earth was still very soft. When he reached the Cherokee Country he was very tired and his giant wings began to flap and strike the ground. When his wings struck the earth there was a valley and where they turned up again there was a mountain. The animals above, seeing this, were afraid that the whole world would be mountains so they called the grandfather buzzard back to the sky vault, but the heart of the Cherokee Country is full of mountains to this day.

When the earth was dry and the animals came down, it was still dark, so they got the sun and set it in a track to go every day across the island from east to west. At first the sun was so close that all the animals like to have burned up. Tsiska'gili, the Red Crawfish, had his shell scorched a bright red so that his meat was spoiled. And to this day the Cherokee will not eat the meat of the Red Crawfish.

The conjure men put the sun another handbreadth higher in the air but it was still too hot. They raised it another and yet again until they had raised it just under the sky arch. Then it was right and they left it so. This is why the conjurers call the highest place Gulkwa'gine Di'galun'latiyun; "the seventh height," because it is seven handbreadths above the earth. Every day the sun goes along its track and at night returns to its starting place.

There is another world under this that is just like ours except that the winters are when we are having summer and the summers are when we are having winter. The streams that come down from the high mountain tops are the trails by which we can reach this underworld and the springs at the heads of these streams are the doorways by which we enter. But no one can go to this world without first being purified and fasting for a long time. He must also have for a guide one of the people who live in the other world. We know that the seasons are different in this other world because the water in the springs is always warmer in the winter and cooler than the outer air in the summer.

When the animals and plants were first made—we do not know by whom—they were told by the Great One to watch and keep awake for seven nights just as the young men fast and keep awake when they pray for their medicine to work. The plants and animals tried to do this and nearly all were awake through the first night, but the next night several dropped off to sleep and then others as time went on until on the seventh night only the owl and the panther and one or two others were yet awake. To these animals the Great One gave the power to see at night and be able to prey on those that had fallen asleep and now must forever sleep, soon after the sun goes down. Of the trees only the cedar, the pine, the spruce, the holly, and the laurel were awake to the end and to them it was given to be always green and to be the best for making medicine. But to the others it was said, "Because you have not endured to the end you shall lose your hair every winter."

Before the world was dry enough for all the people and animals to come down and live on it, all things lived and talked in common. It was said by the myth keepers that when man was first created that there were only a brother and sister, but that one day he struck her with a fish and she bore a child and every seven days another until there was danger that there would not be enough room for all the new people, so it was then made that a woman would only bring forth a child once every year.

The Rattlesnake's Vengeance

ONE DAY in the old times when we could still talk with other creatures, while some children were playing about the house, their mother inside heard them scream. Running out she found that a rattlesnake had crawled from the grass, and taking up a stick she killed it.

The father was out hunting in the mountains, and that evening when coming home after dark through the gap he heard a strange wailing sound. Looking about he found that he had come into the midst of a whole company of rattlesnakes, which all had their mouths open and seemed to be crying. He asked them the reason for their trouble, and they told him that his own wife that day killed their chief, the Yellow Rattlesnake, and they were just now about to send the Black Rattlesnake to their revenge.

The hunter said he was very sorry, but they told him that if he spoke the truth he must be ready to make satisfaction and give his wife as a sacrifice for the life of their chief. Not knowing what might happen otherwise, he consented. They then told him that the Black Rattlesnake would go home with him and coil up just outside the door in the dark. He must go inside where he would find his wife awaiting him, and ask her to get him a drink of fresh water from the spring. That was all.

He went home and knew that the Black Rattlesnake was following. It was night when he arrived and very dark, but he found his wife waiting with his supper ready. He sat down

and asked for a drink of water. She handed him a gourd full from the jar, but he said he wanted it fresh from the spring, so she took a bowl and went out of the door.

The next moment he heard a cry, and going out he found that the Black Rattlesnake had bitten her and that she was already dying. He stayed with her until she was dead, when the Black Rattlesnake came out from the grass again and said his tribe was not satisfied.

He then taught the hunter a prayer song, and said, "When you meet any of us hereafter sing this song and we shall not hurt you; but if by accident one of us should bite one of your people then sing this song over him and he will recover." And the Cherokee have kept the song to this day.

How The Milky Way Came To Be

A LONG TIME AGO in the Cherokee country, when the sky was all clear at night except for a few stars, there lived an old man and an old woman who made their living by beating meal and selling it to the other villagers for meat and skins.

Then one year late in the fall they noticed that something

had been stealing some of their meal at night. They became alarmed because they knew that none of the villagers would steal their meal. They looked around the house and then around the meal pounding places and finally found the track of a giant dog.

When they looked at the track they became afraid because they had never seen so big a dog track before. They thought about the size of the track and discussed the theft of the meal all day but did not decide to do anything about it that day.

That night the meal again disappeared, so the next day the old people called a meeting or a family council to see what was to be done about the giant dog. Now one, and then another, rose to speak and tell what he would do with the dog, but always the family disapproved because every one was afraid of hurting a dog that undoubtedly was from another world.

At last the old one said that he thought everyone should bring noise makers to the house in which he lived. Then that night they could all hide around the meal beaters and wait for the giant dog. When the giant dog came they could all rise up and beat their drums and rattles and shout a great deal so that the dog would become so frightened he would never come to the Cherokee country again. The family was very happy because they knew that the old one had found a way to rid them of the thief.

When the stars were bright, and Sister Moon had made her way half across the sky vault, the dog was seen by the family, approaching from the west. He was a great dog in size and his coat shone silver in the moonlight. When he came to the meal pounders he began to eat the meal in great gulps so that the old one was afraid, but he finally gave a shout as a signal and all the family rose and began making a tremendous lot of noise.

They shouted and shook their rattles and pounded their drums until the noise rolled up the mountain like a great thunder. The dog, hearing all this, became frightened and confused so that he ran around and around within the circle of the shouting people. Then he gave a great leap into the sky, and the meal pouring out of his mouth made a white trail across the sky. That is where we can see the Milky Way which the Cherokee call to this day Gil' LiUtsun'Stanun'yi, "Where the dog ran."

Why The Possum's Tail Is Bare

THE POSSUM used to have a long, bushy tail, and was so proud of it that he combed it every morning and sang about it at the dance, until the Rabbit, who had no tail since the Bear pulled it out, became very jealous and made up his mind to play the Possum a trick.

There was to be a great council and dance at which all the animals were to be present. It was the Rabbit's business to send out the news, so as he was passing the possum's place he stopped to ask him if he intended to be there.

The Possum said he would come if he could have a special seat, "Because I have such a handsome tail that I ought to sit

where everybody can see me." The Rabbit promised to attend to it and to send someone besides to comb and dress the Possum's tail for the dance, so the Possum was very much pleased and agreed to come.

Then the Rabbit went over to the Cricket, who is such an expert hair cutter that the Indians called him the barber, and told him to go next morning and dress the Possum's tail for the dance that night. He told the Cricket just what to do and then went on about some other mischief.

In the morning the Cricket went to the Possum's house and said he had come to get him ready for the dance. So the Possum stretched himself out and shut his eyes while the Cricket combed out his tail and wrapped a red string around it to keep it smooth until night. But all the time, as he wound the string around, he was clipping off the hair close to the roots and the Possum never knew it.

When it was night the Possum went to the townhouse where the dance was to be and found the best seat ready for him, just as the Rabbit had promised. When his turn came in the dance he loosened the string from his tail and stepped into the middle of the floor. The drummers began to drum and the Possum began to sing, "See my beautiful tail."

Everybody shouted and he danced around the circle and sang again, "See what a fine color it has." They shouted again and he danced around another time, "See how it sweeps the ground."

The animals shouted more loudly than ever, and the Possum was delighted. He danced around again and sang, "See how fine the fur is." Then everybody laughed so long that the Possum wondered what they meant. He looked around the circle of animals and they were all laughing at him.

Then he looked down at his beautiful tail and saw that there was not a hair left upon it, but that it was as bare as the tail of a lizard. He was so much astonished and ashamed that he could not say a word, but rolled over helpless on the ground and grinned as the Possum does to this day when taken by surprise.

Ataga'hi The Magic Lake

WESTWARD from the headwaters of Oconaluftee river, in the wildest depths of the Great Smoky Mountains, which form the line between North Carolina and Tennessee, is the enchanted lake of Ataga'hi, "Gall place." Although all the Cherokee know that it is there, no one has ever seen it.

Should a stray hunter come near the place he would know it by the whirring sound of thousands of wild ducks flying about

the lake. But on reaching the spot he would find only a dry flat, without bird or animals or blade of grass, unless he had first sharpened his spiritual vision by prayer and fasting and an all-night vigil.

Because it is not seen, some people think the lake has dried up long ago, but this is not true. To one who kept watch and fasted through the night it would appear at daybreak as a wide-extending but shallow sheet of purple water, fed by springs spouting from high cliffs around.

In the water are all kinds of fish and reptiles, and swimming upon the surface or flying overhead are great flocks of ducks and pigeons, while all about the shores are bear tracks crossing in every direction.

It is the medicine lake of the birds and animals. Whenever a bear is wounded by the hunters he makes his way through the woods to this lake and plunges into the water, and when he comes out upon the other side his wounds are healed.

But for this reason the animals keep the lake invisible to the hunters.

The Race Between The Crane and The Hummingbird

THE HUMMINGBIRD and the Crane were both in love with a pretty woman. She preferred the Hummingbird, who was as handsome as the Crane was awkward, but the Crane was so persistent that in order to get rid of him she finally told him he must challenge the other to a race and she would marry the winner.

The Hummingbird was so swift—almost like a flash of lightning—and the Crane was so slow and heavy, that she felt sure the Hummingbird would win. She did not know the Crane could fly all night.

They agreed to start from her house and fly around the circle of the world to the beginning, and the one who came in first would marry the woman.

At the word, the Hummingbird darted off like an arrow and was out of sight in a moment, leaving his rival to follow heavily behind. He flew all day, and when evening came he stopped to roost for the night. He was far ahead.

But the Crane flew steadily all night, passing the Hummingbird soon after midnight and going on until he came to a creek and stopped to rest about daylight. The Hummingbird woke up in the morning and flew on again, thinking how easily he would win the race, until he reached the creek and there found the Crane spearing tadpoles with his long bill, for breakfast. He was very much surprised and wondered how this could have happened, but he flew swiftly by and soon left the Crane out of sight again.

The Crane finished his breakfast and started on, and when evening came he kept on as before. This time it was hardly midnight when he passed the Hummingbird asleep on a limb, and in the morning he had finished his breakfast before the other came up. The next day he gained a little more, and on the fourth day he was spearing tadpoles for dinner when the Hummingbird passed him.

On the fifth and sixth days it was late in the afternoon before the Hummingbird came up, and on the morning of the seventh day the Crane was a whole night's travel ahead. He took his time at breakfast and then fixed himself up nicely as he could at the creek and came in at the starting place where the woman lived, early in the morning.

When the Hummingbird arrived in the afternoon he found that he had lost the race, but the woman declared she would never have such an ugly fellow as the Crane for a husband, so she stayed single.

Why The Buzzard's Head Is Bare

THE BUZZARD used to have a fine topknot. He was so proud of it that he refused to eat carrion, and while the other birds were pecking at the body of a Deer or other animal which they had found he would strut around and say. "You may have it all. It is not good enough for me."

They resolved to punish him, and with the help of the Buffalo carried out a plot by which the Buzzard lost not his topknot alone, but nearly all the feathers on his head. He lost his pride at the same time, so that he is willing enough now to eat carrion for a living.

Why The Mink Smells

The Mink was such a great thief that at last the animals held a council about the matter. It was decided to burn him, so they caught the Mink, built a great fire and threw him into it.

As the blaze went up and they smelt the roasted flesh, they began to think he was punished enough and would probably do better in the future, so they took him out of the fire. But the Mink was already burned black and is black ever since, and whenever he is attacked or excited he smells again like roasted meat.

The lesson did no good, however, and he is still as great a thief as ever.

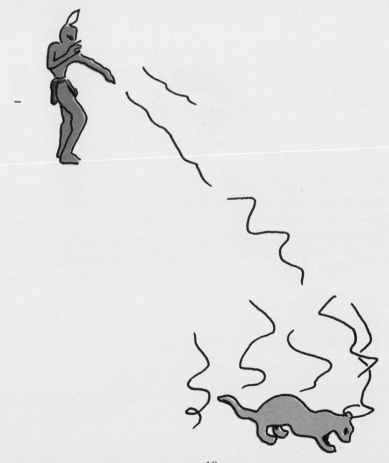

Cherokee Indian Ball Game

LONG AGO Cherokee Indian Ball was played to decide which village or town was supreme in the ungentle art of mayhem on the ball field.

The two teams gathered from their respective townships on a large field, usually beside some flowing mountain stream. The first act was to set up their goal post at each end of the field. Then they marked the mid point in between. This done, the two teams proceeded to pair off into individual opponents. When all the pairing off was done the referee threw the ball up between the two captains and the mad scramble was on. Anything went —biting, choking, gouging, scratching, twisting arms and legs— even banging each other on the head with their wooden rackets.

The object of the game was to carry the ball between the goal post twelve times. The first team to have twelve counting pegs stuck in the ground by the medicine man won the ball game. There was no time out, nor substitution. If a player was knocked out—and they often were—his opponent also left the game. Twenty men might start the game and only a few finish it.

Sometimes a game might last until dark if the two teams were well matched. There was no time limit on how long a game could last. Once it started it was never over until one team had scored twelve points.

In olden days Indians gathered from miles around to watch the games and bet anything they possessed on their favorite team. It was not uncommon for a man to go home after a game minus both the horse he rode and the shirt he wore.

THE TRAIL OF TEARS

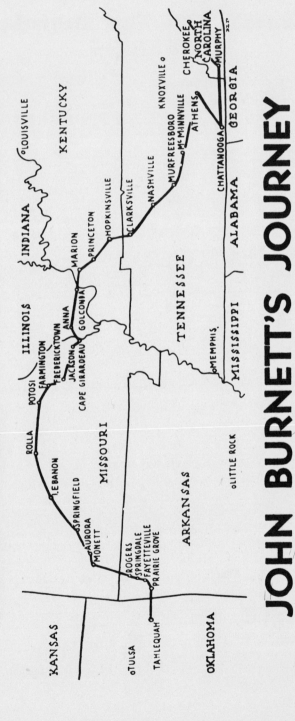

JOHN BURNETT'S JOURNEY

Removal Of The Cherokees 1838-39

Birthday Story of Private John G. Burnett, Captain Abraham McClellan's Company, 2nd Regiment, 2nd Brigade, Mounted Infantry, Cherokee Indian Removal 1838-39.

Children;

This is my birthday December the 11th 1890, I am eighty years old today. I was born at Kings Iron Works in Sullivan County, Tennessee, December the 11th, 1810. I grew into manhood fishing in Beaver Creek and roaming through the forest hunting the Deer the wild Boar and the timber Wolf. Often spending weeks at a time in the solitary wilderness with no companions but my rifle, hunting knife, and a small hatchet that I carried in my belt in all of my wilderness wanderings.

On these long hunting trips I met and became acquainted with many of the Cherokee Indians, hunting with them by day and sleeping around their camp fires by night. I learned to speak their language, and they taught me the arts of trailing and building traps and snares. On one of my long hunts in the fall of 1829 I found a young Cherokee who had been shot by a roving band of hunters and who had eluded his pursuers and concealed himself under a shelving rock. Weak from loss of blood the poor creature was unable to walk and almost famished for water. I carried him to a spring bathed and bandaged the bullet wound, built a shelter out of bark peeled from a dead chestnut tree. Nursed and protected him feeding him on chestnuts and roasted deer meat. When he was able to travel I accompanied him to the home of his people and remained so long that I was given up for lost. By this time I had become an expert rifleman and fairly good archer and a good trapper and spent most of my time in the forest in quest of game.

The removal of the Cherokee Indians from their life long homes in the year of 1838 found me a young man in the prime of life and a Private soldier in the American Army. Being acquainted with many of the Indians and able to fluently speak their language, I was sent as interpreter into the Smoky Mountain Country in May, 1838, and witnessed the execution of the most brutal order in the History of American Warfare. I saw the helpless Cherokees arrested and dragged from their homes, and driven at the bayonet point into the stockades. And in the chill of a drizzling rain on an October morning I saw them loaded like cattle or sheep into six hundred and forty-five wagons and started toward the west.

One can never forget the sadness and solemnity of that morning. Chief John Ross led in prayer and when the bugle sounded and the wagons started rolling many of the children rose to their feet and waved their little hands good-by to their mountain homes, knowing they were leaving them forever. Many of these helpless people did not have blankets and many of them had been driven from home barefooted.

On the morning of November the 17th we encountered a terrific sleet and snow storm with freezing temperatures and from that day until we reached the end of the fateful journey on March the 26th 1839, the sufferings of the Cherokees were awful. The trail of the exiles was a trail of death. They had to sleep in the wagons and on the ground without fire. And I have known as many as twenty-two of them to die in one night of pneumonia due to ill treatment, cold, and exposure. Among this number was the beautiful Christian wife of Chief John Ross. This noble hearted woman died a martyr to childhood, giving her only blanket for the protection of a sick child. She rode thinly clad through a blinding sleet and snow storm, developed pneumonia and died in the still hours of a bleak winter night, with her head resting on Lieutenant Greggs saddle blanket.

I made the long journey to the west with the Cherokees and did all that a Private soldier could do to alleviate their sufferings. When on guard duty at night I have many times walked my beat in my blouse in order that some sick child might have the warmth of my overcoat.

I was on guard duty the night Mrs. Ross died. When relieved at midnight I did not retire, but remained around the wagon out of sympathy for Chief Ross, and at daylight was detailed by Captain McClellan to assist in the burial like the other unfortunates who died on the way. Her uncoffined body was buried in a shallow grave by the roadside far from her native mountain home, and the sorrowing Cavalcade moved on.

Being a young man I mingled freely with the young women and girls. I have spent many pleasant hours with them when I was supposed to be under my blanket, and they have many times sung their mountain songs for me, this being all that they could do to repay my kindness. And with all my association with Indian girls from October 1829 to March 26th 1839, I did not meet one who was a moral prostitute. They are kind and tender hearted and many of them are beautiful.

The only trouble that I had with anybody on the entire journey to the west was a brutal teamster by the name of Ben McDonal, who was using his whip on an old feeble Cherokee to hasten him into the wagon. The sight of that old and nearly blind creature quivering under the lashes of a bull whip was too much for me. I attempted to stop McDonal and it ended in a personal encounter. He lashed me across the face, the wire tip on his whip cutting a bad gash in my cheek. The little hatchet that I had carried in my hunting days was in my belt, and McDonal was carried unconscious from the scene.

I was placed under guard but, Ensign Henry Bullock and Private Elkanah Millard had both witnessed the encounter. They gave Captain McClellan the facts and I was never brought to trial. Years later I met 2nd Lieutenant Riley and Ensign Bullock at Bristol at John Robersons show, and Bullock jokingly reminded me that there was a case still pending against me before a court martial and wanted to know how much longer I was going to have the trial put off?

McDonal finally recovered, and in the year 1851, was running on a boat out of Memphis, Tennessee.

The long painful journey to the west ended March 26th, 1839, with four-thousand silent graves reaching from the foot hills of the Smoky Mountains to what is known as Indian territory in the West. And covetousness on the part of the white race was the cause of all that the Cherokees had to suffer.

Ever since Ferdinand Desoto, made his journey through the Indian country in the year of 1540, there had been a tradition of a rich Gold mine somewhere in the Smoky Mountain Country, and I think the tradition was true. At a·festival at Echata on Christmas night 1829, I danced and played with Indian girls who were wearing ornaments around their necks that looked Gold.

In the year of 1828, a little Indian boy living on Ward creek had sold a Gold nugget to a white trader, and that nugget sealed the doom of the Cherokees. In a short time the country was over run with Armed brigands claiming to be Government Agents, who paid no attention to the rights of the Indians who were the legal possessors of the country. Crimes were committed that were a disgrace to civilization. Men were shot in cold blood, lands were confiscated. Homes were burned and the inhabitants driven out by these Gold hungry brigands.

Chief Junaluska was personally acquainted with President Andrew Jackson. Junaluska had taken five-hundred of the flower of his Cherokee scouts and helped Jackson to win the battle of the Horse Shoe leaving thirty-three of them dead on the field. And in that battle Junaluska had drove his Tomahawk through the skull of a Creek warrior, when the Creek had Jackson at mercy.

Chief John Ross sent Junaluska as an envoy to plead with President Jackson for protection for his people, but Jackson's manner was cold and indifferent toward the rugged son of the forest who had saved his life. He met Junaluska heard his plea but curtly said "Sir your audience is ended, there is nothing I can do for you." The doom of the Cherokee was sealed, Washington D. C. had decreed that they must be driven West, and their lands given to the white man, and in May 1838 an Army of four thousand regulars, and three thousand volunteer soldiers under command of General Winfield Scott, marched into the Indian country and wrote the blackest chapter on the pages of American History.

Men working in the fields were arrested and driven to the stockades. Women were dragged from their homes by soldiers whose language they could not understand. Children were often separated from their parents and driven into the stockades with the sky for a blanket and the earth for a pillow. And often the old and infirm were prodded with bayonets to hasten them to the stockades.

In one home death had come during the night, a little sad faced child had died and was lying on a bear skin couch and some women were preparing the little body for burial. All were arrested and driven out leaving the child in the cabin. I don't know who buried the body.

In another home was a frail Mother, apparently a widow and three small children, one just a baby. When told that she must go the Mother gathered the children at her feet, prayed an humble prayer in her native tongue, patted the old family dog on the head, told the faithful creature good-by, with a baby strapped on her back and leading a child with each hand started on her exile. But the task was too great for that frail Mother. A stroke of heart failure relieved her sufferings. She sunk and died with her baby on her back, and her other two children clinging to her hands.

Chief Junaluska who had saved President Jackson's life at the battle of Horse Shoe witnessed this scene, the tears gushing down his cheeks and lifting his cap he turned his face toward the Heavens and said "Oh my God if I had known at the battle of the Horse Shoe what I know now American History would have been differently written."

At this time 1890 we are too near the removal of the Cherokees for our young people to fully understand the enormity of the crime that was committed against a helpless race, truth is the facts are being concealed from the young people of today. School children of today do not know that we are living on lands that were taken from a helpless race at the bayonet point to satisfy the white man's greed for gold.

Future generations will read and condemn the act and I do hope posterity will remember that private soldiers like myself, and like the four Cherokees who were forced by General Scott, to shoot an Indian Chief and his children had to execute the orders of our superiors. We had no choice in the matter.

Twenty-five years after the removal it was my privilege to meet a large company of the Cherokees in uniform of the Confederate Army under Command of Colonel Thomas, they were encamped at Zollicoffer I went to see them. Most of them were just boys at the time of the removal but they instantly recognized me as "the soldier that was good to us." Being able to talk to them in their native language I had an enjoyable day with them. From them I learned that Chief John Ross was still ruler of the nation in 1863. And I wonder if he is still living? He was a noble hearted fellow and suffered a lot for his race.

At one time he was arrested and thrown into a dirty jail in an effort to break his spirit, but he remained true to his people and led them in prayer when they started on their exile. And his Christian wife sacrificed her life for a little girl who had pneumonia. The Anglo Saxon race would build a towering monument to perpetuate her noble act in giving her only blanket for comfort of a sick child. Incidentally the child recovered, but Mrs. Ross is sleeping in an unmarked grave far from her native Smoky Mountain home.

When Scott invaded the Indian country some of the Cherokees fled to caves and dens in the mountains and were never captured and they are there today. I have long intended going there and trying to find them but I have put off going from year to year and now I am too feeble to ride that far. The fleeting years have come and gone and old age has overtaken me, I can truthfully say that neither my rifle, nor my knife are stained with Cherokee blood.

I can truthfully say that I did my best for them when they certainly did need a friend. Twenty-five years after the removal I still lived in their Memory as "the soldier who was good to us."

However murder is murder whether committed by the villian skulking in the dark or by uniformed men stepping to the strains of martial music.

Murder is murder and somebody must answer, somebody must explain the streams of blood that flowed in the Indian country in the summer of 1838. Somebody must explain the four-thousand silent graves that mark the trail of the Cherokees to their exile. I wish I could forget it all, but the picture of six-hundred and forty-five wagons lumbering over the frozen ground with their Cargo of suffering humanity still lingers in my memory.

Let the Historian of a future day tell the sad story with its sighs its tears and dying groans. Let the great Judge of all the earth weigh our actions and reward us according to our work.

Children—Thus ends my promised birthday story. This December the 11th 1890.

The Katydid's Warning

Two hunters camping in the woods were preparing supper one night when a Katydid began singing near them. One of them said sneeringly, "Ku' it sings and doesn't know that it will die before the season ends."

The Katydid answered: "Ku! nive. Oh, so you say. But you need not boast. You will die before tomorrow night." The next day they were surprised by the enemy. The hunter who sneered at the Katydid was killed.

The First Fire

IN THE BEGINNING there was no fire, and the world was cold, until the Thunders (Ani'Hylun'tikwala), who lived up in Galun'lati sent their lightning and put fire into the bottom of a hollow sycamore tree which grew on an island.

The animals knew it was there, because they could see the smoke coming out of the top, but they could not get to it on account of the water, so they held a council to decide what to do. This was a long time ago.

Every animal that could fly or swim was anxious to go after the fire. The Raven offered, and because he was so large and strong they thought he could surely do the work, so he was sent first. He flew high and far across the water and alighted on the sycamore tree, but while he was wondering what to do next, the heat had scorched all his feathers black, and he was frightened and came back without the fire.

The little Screech-Owl (Wa'huhu') volunteered to go, and reached the place safely, but while he was looking down into the hollow tree a blast of hot air came up and nearly burned out his eyes. He managed to fly home as best he could, but it was a long time before he could see well, and his eyes are red to this day.

Then the Hooting Owl (U'guku') and the Horned Owl (Tskili') went, but by the time they got to the hollow tree the fire was burning so fiercely that the smoke nearly blinded them, and the ashes carried up by the wind made white rings about their eyes. They had to come home again without the fire, but with all their rubbing they were never able to get rid of the white rings.

Now no more of the birds would venture, and so the little Uksu'hi snake, the black racer, said he would go through the water and bring back some fire. He swam across to the island and crawled through the grass to the trees, and went in by a small hole at the bottom.

The heat and smoke were too much for him, too. After dodging about blindly over the hot ashes until he was almost on fire himself he managed by good luck to get out again at the same hole, but his body had been scorched black, and he has ever since had the habit of darting and doubling on his tracks as if trying to escape from close quarters.

He came back and the great blacksnake, Gule'gi, "The Climber," offered to go for fire. He swam over to the island and climbed up the tree on the outside, as the blacksnake always does, but when he put his head down into the hole the smoke choked him so that he fell into the burning stump, and before he could climb out again he was as black as the Uksu'hi.

Now they held another council, for there still was no fire, and the world was cold, but birds, snakes, and four-footed animals, all had some excuse for not going, because they were all afraid to venture near the burning sycamore, until at last Kanane'ski amai'yehi, the Water Spider, said she would go.

This is not the water spider that looks like a mosquito, but the other one, with black downy hair and red stripes on her body. She can run on top of the water or dive to the bottom, so there would be no trouble to get over to the island, but the question was, how could she bring back the fire?

"I'll manage that," said the Water Spider; so she spun a thread from her body and wove it into a tusti bowl, which she fastened on her back. Then she crossed over to the island and through the grass to where the fire was still burning. She put one little coal of fire into her bowl. And the Water Spider still keeps her tusti bowl.

The Museum of the Cherokee Indian

THE MUSEUM is located in Cherokee, North Carolina, U. S. Highway 441.

Here under one roof has been collected the finest display of Cherokee Indian artifacts in existence. Rescued from burial grounds and ancient camp sites dating back 10,000 years, these artifacts trace the Red Man's history from the time of the Dawn Age to the present.

In modern museum technique, artifacts of cane, stone, bone, shell and wood have been arranged to spell out in simplicity the story of the Cherokee Indian.

The Museum is owned and operated by the Cherokee Historical Association, producer of the Indian Drama *Unto These Hills,* and of Oconaluftee Indian Village recreating Cherokee life of 200 years ago. This non-profit corporation chartered by the State of North Carolina is governed by a trustee board of Cherokee and white citizens of the state. Proceeds go into preserving the history and enlarging the opportunities for the Cherokee area.

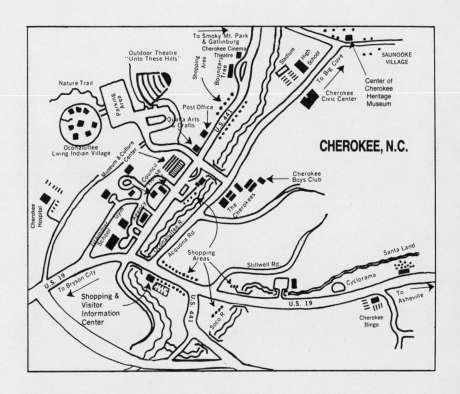